Guide for Simple Luxury

Elevate Your Everyday
Without Breaking the Bank

To you an abundant life
comms

Connie Paradise

Guide for SIMPLE LUXURIES

Elevate Your Everyday Without Breaking the Bank

CONNIE PARADISE

Connie Paradise

A Guide for Simple Luxuries:
Elevate Your Every Day Without Breaking the Bank

Published in the United States by Connie Paradise Media, LLC
First Edition

Photography by Connie Paradise

Cover Design by Meredith Hancock

ISBN9798878208338 (Paperback)

Praise for
Guide for Simple Luxuries

Connie's *Guide for Simple Luxuries* is an enjoyable read that takes me back to a time when life was simpler. It is an excellent reminder of how we can enjoy life's everyday luxuries by making simple changes with a positive mindset. Her storytelling style adds to the book's charm.

> SHARON FARINHOLT, author
> realtor, The Marathon of Running
> a Business

Connie's passion and wisdom for living a vibrant life shine through this beautiful guide. She redefines luxury as an emotion you feel when you create space to savor and appreciate what matters most in your life. You will be inspired to implement the tools in this book to create your own luxurious life.

> TAMARA WOLFE, speaker,
> life coach, author
> Short, Sweet, and Sacred

Connie's book offers a fresh take on the true meaning of luxury — living intentionally and celebrating the small things that define our quality of life. She offers everything from practical tips about transforming our homes to make us feel good to the importance of good manners. Her book reminds us to look around, pay attention, and be inspired to create the life we want. An easy read, this little book is a treasure trove of valuable life lessons, profound wisdom, and contagious positivity — something we all deserve to give ourselves.

> BARBARA QUAST, Designer
> Quast Interior Designs

In this captivating book, Connie embarks on a journey that unveils the secrets and art of living a truly luxurious life. In today's fast-paced, instant-access world, it is easy to get caught up in the chaos of everyday life, forgetting to savor the finer things that life has to offer. This book reminds us to pause, take a breath, and relish in the exquisite moments that enrich our lives. *Guide for Simple Luxuries* goes beyond material possessions and tangible experiences to encourage a mindset that builds on self-care, self-love, and personal fulfillment. Through expert advice and inspiring stories, Connie unveils the secrets to living an intentionally luxurious life. Prepare to indulge your senses, challenge your perceptions, and unlock the doors to a world where luxury knows no boundaries. Connie will inspire you to live life extraordinarily.

CRYSTEL LYNN SMITH,
business coach, speaker, author,
Business 101 and Today I Am Grateful

CONTENTS

To Mom. My biggest fan who showed
me strength through her style and
grace. I love and admire you.

Luxury
is a state of mind.

~L'Wren Scott

Introduction

Extravagant jewelry, speedy cars, lavish vacations, high-end fashion, and fine dining are the things we usually associate with luxury. These beautiful material possessions are commonly seen as symbols of wealth and require a substantial income. Many seem to long for them but may not have the resources to live this extravagant lifestyle.

As you continue reading, you'll discover that luxury encompasses more than just material possessions and can be expressed in various ways. You may be surprised at how much happiness, serenity, and fulfillment you can experience without an opulent existence. The essence of luxury is all about indulging in unnecessary experiences that evoke pleasurable emotions. It's like treating yourself to something that makes you feel good and uplifts your spirits, even if not a necessity. These can be found anywhere!

In the hustle and bustle of modern life, it can be challenging to distinguish what holds real significance amid the clutter that many of us accumulate. While we may appreciate the ability to purchase things, it raises the question: do we genuinely require them? Why are we buying them? What is the financial and emotional cost?

Although some argue that luxuries are unnecessary for a fulfilling life, they can offer benefits by stimulating and creatively expressing our spirits, adding to the joy, love, and peace we experience. Material possessions do not solely define luxury, as we often accumulate too much, leading to complications in our lives. It is also about making daily routines and experiences feel magical and essential for our emotional well-being. We can adjust our practices and change our thinking to find beauty in everything.

I make it a daily practice to seek out the little things that make life special. Whether it's a stunning sunset or a simple act of kindness, I believe finding beauty in our surroundings can truly enhance our lives. This includes working on myself and striving to be better each day. When I appreciate things for what they are, it lifts my mood and attracts positivity. When I treat myself well, the days become more pleasant, my creative thinking is enhanced, and I can maintain a more consistent level of happiness that positively affects every aspect of my life. I look for ways to improve my surroundings and make life more fulfilling.

I see simple luxuries all around; many don't involve spending money. Sometimes, it requires saving money, like being debt-free. I am anxious to share my personal experience and knowledge regarding the benefits of adding small luxuries to your daily routine. Doing so can help shift your mindset from scarcity to abundance and ultimately improve your mood. I don't have to look elsewhere for fulfillment and satisfaction when my mind is elevated. So many simple and cost-effective solutions can help you achieve that.

My book aims to redefine luxury by separating it from financial wealth and instead offer advice and concepts to intentionally create a daily environment that is comfortable, enjoyable, and convenient without spending a lot. The ideas are non-essential; you could live without them, but why should you? They will elevate your everyday life and cultivate a positive environment that brings you joy if you use and practice them.

I started playing the piano again because I enjoy it, not because I think I have a chance of winning an impressive award. The fact that I could still read music years after I took lessons in elementary school gave me a thrill. After a month or so of practice, my fingers remembered the keys, and the subsequent sessions have given me great satisfaction and happiness. I make it a point to practice 20 minutes a day for relaxation. Appreciating the small luxuries in life can provide much-needed rest and rejuvenation, giving you the energy to achieve even greater things.

Connie Paradise

Chapter 1

REDEFINING LUXURY

Valuing Being Over Buying

According to Webster's dictionary, luxury is the enjoyment of something that brings pleasure, satisfaction, or comfort. From an emotional perspective, the meaning of luxury can vary from one person to another. What is revered by one can be meaningless to another. More important is to recognize that luxury isn't solely determined by one's income or the amount of money you spend. To explore the idea of redefining luxury, we will examine the impact of mindset and perspective.

For instance, a new mom might consider a simple afternoon nap a luxury, while a frequent business traveler may feel a home-cooked meal a treat. Similarly, a young woman working long hours to climb the corporate ladder may view taking an hour for a mani/pedi as a significant indulgence. Or imagine the feeling of no financial worries. I would say that it is pretty lavish.

Traditionally, an afternoon nap or a trip to a nail salon may not be considered luxurious. Still, for many individuals in these same circumstances, the experience results in feelings of pleasure and comfort. I know for sure that my husband, Ollin, thinks quite highly of 40 winks on a Sunday afternoon and considers it a luxury since he has absolutely zero chance of it happening during the week.

Luxury is subjective and depends on personal feelings. But the results aren't necessarily positive when money is involved. Anticipating pleasure from something you can't afford can lead to disappointment and wasted money in the end.

Nailya Ordabayeva, an associate professor of marketing at Boston College Carroll School of Management and the author of a study, reported to CNBC Make It that purchasing luxury goods can boost one's self-esteem, confidence, satisfaction, and social status from an emotional standpoint.

According to Ordabayeva, consumers are drawn to luxury when feeling less confident or powerful, hoping to gain a boost through the purchase. However, not everyone gets the feeling they hoped for; sometimes, it is disappointment and regret.

It's worth noting that what we consider a luxury can change over time. For example, a dishwasher was once

2

considered a luxury for women 50 years ago, and only 11% of American households had dryers in 1960. However, they are now regarded as essential in most homes. Picture living without either appliance today with our busy lives.

Some consider experiences luxuries and prized over material possessions. I've been one of those people. Above my fully stocked wine rack in the corner of my great room hangs a plaque given to me by a friend. It perfectly describes my intentional approach to life and the experiences that I have adopted over the years. My friend recognized my tendency to live to the fullest and wanted to memorialize it on my wall. The quote on the plaque is very personal, as I have enjoyed my fair share of chocolates and wine. I am proud to display it as it reads,

"Life should not be a journey to the grave with the intention of arriving safely in a well-preserved body, but rather to skid in sideways, chocolate in one hand, wine in the other, body is thoroughly worn out and screaming, "Woo Hoo, what a ride."

As women, it can be challenging to prioritize intentional living and being present in the moment, mainly if you are responsible for other's care. My son is grown with children, so I have lived through it and understand the challenges. However, I did take moments to revive myself so that I could carry on my responsibilities.

Even when we do manage to set aside time for ourselves, we're often too tired to relish it fully. Life shouldn't be a never-ending juggling act trying to keep all the plates spinning. Instead, we should make time to savor experiences and find joy in the simple things rather than relying on costly material possessions that some are constantly running after. Shifting to an appreciation for the things we have access to triggers positive feelings. I remember a verse I read long ago that I keep in mind — Gratitude turns what we have into enough. More about gratitude later.

Most women have prioritized their loved ones at their own expense, prioritizing other's needs above their own. Take charge with intention and carve out time for yourself to recharge.

Living intentionally involves making decisions aligned with our values, beliefs, and goals. It means avoiding impulsive choices and making deliberate decisions that positively impact our lives. With this in mind, taking small steps to bring comfort and convenience into our lives can help elevate our mood and emotions to a higher level, attracting more positivity and setting the tone for days to come.

Living intentionally starts with deliberately selecting the kind of life you want to lead, the people you want to surround yourself with, and the level of involvement you desire from them. Once you have made these decisions, pursue them with enthusiasm and courage. Earlier in my life, I was clear about my ambitions and sought opportunities to make them a reality. I wanted experiences.

During several jobs, I had the opportunity to travel extensively, sometimes accompanied by my bosses. On a trip to Seattle, we checked into the Four Seasons, a stunning property with immaculate floors, elegant

4

wooden walls, splendid flower arrangements, and a dazzling infinity pool with breathtaking views of Elliott Bay. As we entered the lobby and I soaked in the atmosphere, I casually remarked to my boss, "This is how I believe I was meant to be treated." He chuckled the way he often did, but I was serious. My passion for traveling led me to seek jobs that would take me across the country and many exotic islands for conferences. I had the opportunity to dine at top-notch restaurants in places I never thought I'd visit, and I saw sights that left me in awe. These trips were all part of my work responsibilities.

Although I already had a lovely home, a few experiences during that time made me realize that it was possible to make my home and life even more exceptional without spending a lot of money. I longed for an aesthetically pleasing and comfy space to live in and held an image of that home.

I discovered a charming first-floor condo resembling a carriage house with a private courtyard just outside Washington, DC. I swear that I attracted this home into my life because it matched the image I held in my mind for a long time. The same can be said for the jobs that came after, as they perfectly fit my skill set.

Thanks to my frequent business travel, I was able to rack up quite a collection of frequent flyer points, which I happily put towards some amazing personal vacations all around the world. I coupled them with points from the credit card I charged all my personal purchases, and I traveled to places I only dreamed about. Whenever I felt the urge to go, I closed my door and set out on a journey at a moment's notice. This was just one example of how I found luxurious experiences without spending too much money.

Redefining luxury means that rather than following the traditional approach, we strive to incorporate small moments of appreciation into our daily lives. I appreciated every one of those trips and took time to savor the sites, the kindness of the people I met, and the opportunities presented. The goal is to shift our perspective and place value on these meaningful moments.

In our fast-paced society, it can be challenging to sort through what truly matters amidst the overwhelming number of worldly possessions and clutter many of us own. Although we may be grateful for having the financial means to acquire things, it begs the question: do we really need them? Why do we acquire all this stuff, and what's the reason behind it?

A recent Forbes article suggests marketers, advertisers, corporations, or capitalism are to blame. True? We are solely deciding to pull out our credit cards when it comes time to buy. What compels us to buy things that we don't need in the first place? The article cited several reasons for the purchases we make.

Many of us believe that accumulating possessions is the key to feeling secure. We reason if owning some material possessions can provide us with security, then owning more will bring us even greater security. However, once we have met our basic needs, the actual security that physical possessions provide is less stable than we might think. Possessions can perish, spoil, or fade, and they can disappear more quickly than we realize. This fear of missing out (FOMO) on accumulating possessions can lead to a false sense of security.

More than a few of us believe owning things will bring us joy. Although we may not openly admit it, many seek happiness through material possessions. This leads us to chase after larger homes, faster cars, the latest technology, and fashionable clothing, all in the hope that it will make us happier. However, the happiness that comes from owning physical possessions is often short-lived. It can even cause regret when we realize it let you down rather than lifted you.

Advertising influences us more than we realize. How can it not, with research indicating that we are exposed to around 5,000 ads daily, all promising that our lives will improve if we purchase their products? With so many messages bombarding us from every direction, it's no wonder we start to believe them. Recognizing how much advertising can impact our thoughts and behaviors is important.

Envy is a powerful force for economic activity in affluent societies, making many people aspire to impress others. The term "conspicuous consumption" was coined long ago, but it is more prevalent today than ever before. Once our basic needs are met, consumption becomes more than just fulfilling our needs. Unfortunately, it often becomes a means of displaying our wealth, status, and financial success to the world.

It's natural for us to compare ourselves to others, and what's more, our society encourages this behavior. The prevalence of social media has resulted in increased pressure to maintain appearances. We notice what others buy, wear, and drive, and we often make unnecessary purchases to keep up with our friends. Consider that you may have the wrong friends if you need to impress them with expensive possessions, not your intellectual and emotional contribution to the relationship.

Many try to compensate for our shortcomings by seeking confidence in material possessions like fancy clothes or expensive cars. We also often turn to unnecessary purchases to try and ease feelings of loss, loneliness, or heartache. However, these pursuits could be more fulfilling rather than preventing us from addressing the root of our issues.

Acknowledging a harsh reality, some people possess varying degrees of innate selfish and greedy nature. This is not a trait we are born with but rather one that has been displayed in the past through methods such as force, coercion, dishonesty, and warfare in the pursuit of expanding our realm. Unfortunately, these tendencies are still prevalent in our modern world. Acquiring excess material possessions does not bring true enrichment to our lives, and it can prevent us from experiencing life's actual benefits.

I'll say it again: luxury is not always about the size of your bank account but about recognizing your self-worth and prioritizing treating yourself and those who are important to you well. It is the sensation you experience when engaging in an activity that pleases you, maybe sharing with those you love. Thankfully, it only sometimes demands a large sum of money to be invested. Imagine how you feel taking an hour from your busy schedule to sip a fancy coffee at an outdoor table

Saying yes to what
matters most is living
with intention. You
don't want to waste
a moment of this
precious gift of life.

while reading a few chapters from the riveting novel you picked up from the library this morning, I'd say it's a beautiful way to recharge. As I write this, I'm exhaling a sigh, simply thinking about these moments. You can turn simple activities into luxurious experiences, and here is even better news: you can attract more of them. We'll chat about this later.

Saying yes to what matters most to you is living with intention. Life is fleeting; it's almost like the more we live, the faster it seems to slip away. Don't waste a moment of this precious gift of life with things not high on your priority list. Adding small luxuries to our daily routine can enhance the joy of this beautiful life that we have been given. These little niceties are especially important to lift our spirits in the challenging times when we've reached the end of our rope as we strive for more of the Universe's abundant bounty.

Women have been taught and expected to put everyone else before themselves and only tend to our needs when they are comfortable and met. We spend most of our time doing things for others, and most of us do it because we are born caregivers and nurturers. We love making life comfortable for those we love and often find that we've run out of steam or time to provide for ourselves. This drained feeling points to the age-old metaphor "You can't pour from an empty cup" and emphasizes the importance of rest and time for oneself. Every flight attendant instructs you to equip yourself with oxygen masks before you can help others. In these terms, caring for yourself, then others make sense.

Honestly, simple luxuries are underrated. Our physical, emotional, and mental needs are fueled with small rewards whether or not we realize this. After completing a task, it's essential to take time to reward ourselves. This can be as simple as reflecting on our accomplishments with tea in our favorite cup and saucer or enjoying the freshness and color a small bouquet brings to a room. The refreshing feeling of a daily pick-me-up keeps us going and looking forward with excitement and motivation.

There were times when I lost my passion for life. Sometimes, it became too difficult to continue after putting in so much effort, giving everything I had, and feeling completely exhausted. Simple luxuries allow us to slow down, savor our senses, and find joy in creating the life we want despite everything the world has thrown at us. It is about appreciating life's wonder, magic, surroundings, daily duties, and people. Simple pleasures can bring elegance and beauty to life, enabling you to appreciate the present moment and all that surrounds you.

Luxury is achieving a state of mind where you prioritize and create a life around what you value. It's the art of living quality over quantity, understanding what makes you happy, and savoring the richness of it all. It is an escape that should give you a comfortable feeling. Luxury for me is adding cream instead of milk to my coffee and savoring it while curled up in a comfy leather chair in our sunroom to greet the morning sun.

Not that I wouldn't jump at the chance for a good jaunt through Rome or Paris with a 5-star hotel stopping-off point. I'm just saying that if it's not in your future yet, there is another perspective. Any time you can create a joyous moment for yourself and boost your body's vibration to attract more positivity. (More on this later.) Make the time to treat yourself, be in the moment, and enjoy everyone with appreciation. Even strangers can bring you joy and make every day extraordinary if you let them.

So now comes the time to curate your priorities and define luxury on your terms. This is important, so pay attention. This is where your time and money should go to find the meaningful, good stuff. Remember that caring for yourself and pampering yourself is not selfish. In fact, investing in activities that contribute to your overall well-being is a wise decision. So go ahead. Indulge in some self-care — you deserve it! Your mental and physical health will improve with every change you make. You'll experience increased energy, better stress management, and a reduced risk of illness. Incorporate some of my favorite ways to enjoy simple luxuries into your everyday routine and notice how even the smallest moments become more manageable and enjoyable. Acknowledging your value and prioritizing self-care for a better life is essential.

Ultimately, this chapter aims to redefine luxury as something beyond material wealth. It suggests true luxury is about valuing personal joys, leading an intentional life, and having genuine experiences. By embracing simple pleasures, understanding the negative impact of consumerism, and prioritizing well-being over possessions, we can enrich our lives with true luxury.

This perspective encourages us to cherish life's moments and live authentically, grounded in what genuinely matters. By doing so, we can bring true richness into our lives.

If it doesn't add to
your life, let it go.

Chapter 2

CLEARING THE WAY FOR LUXURY

Clearing Your Home, Clearing Your Mind

There is nothing wrong with material belongings; the Universe wants you to enjoy them from its plentiful bounty. It's when they get out of hand that it's a problem. You cannot uncover and appreciate all your niceties if you can't see them hidden by all you own. Your keys are constantly lost; the dog's leash hides under an accumulation of a week's worth of newspapers, and the suit you planned to wear to the critical meeting tomorrow is at the cleaners.

Living in cluttered surroundings clogs the positive energy flow. Nothing new can flow into your life until you clear a space and make room for it. Simply stated, clutter blocks good things from reaching you. How can you appreciate the beauty of your surroundings if cluttered with stuff that has no meaning for you? Everything cleaned out, organized, and in working order, handy, and freshened up is a simple luxury. Besides giving you a better perspective, clearing clutter saves you time and frustration and opens up new possibilities.

The definition of clutter is items that are no longer useful to you. It could mean you have more than one because they were having a sale on spatulas, and you couldn't resist it. Maybe you don't know what it is or why you bought it, it doesn't fit, you don't like the color, and on and on. It might as well be in the trash if it isn't valuable to you. It can be old or new, but if it has no value to you, it's clutter. Those slacks that don't fit with the price tag still on them are clutter! The manila folder with 10-year-old bank statements is clutter! The cords from the electronics you replaced are nothing but clutter!

Clutter is nothing but stagnated energy, and it says a lot about you and where your life is headed. It is the opposite of luxury and a roadblock to the good things coming your way, while a space free of clutter attracts harmony and abundance into your life.

Many of these things in the store seemed exciting to you but lost their luster once they crossed your threshold. Now, they are hidden out of the way in the "guest bedroom," along with the other boxes and piles of stuff collecting dust.

When you free yourself from clutter, your life becomes manageable. Think about the space this junk takes up in your home, heart, and mind. Trust me, you'll feel liberation and freedom from getting rid of it. Oh, I don't blame you for collecting it all. We are constantly assaulted with ongoing messages telling us what we need. Advertisements are everywhere now, and they make everything look dazzling and irresistible. It appears that advertisers have a better understanding of what you need to improve your quality of life. From this moment on, I permit you to decide for yourself.

Clutter has health implications, too. Clutter can increase stress hormones just from the sheer volume, make it difficult to focus, cause allergies to flare up from the dust, increase the likelihood of slips and falls, and even lead to embarrassment and isolation.

You complain that you can get nothing done, you'll never get organized, nothing motivates you any longer, and you have no idea where to start. Standing in the middle of a hot mess at home feels anything but luxurious. Furthermore, it saps your energy. Clearing clutter is the first step to enjoying the beauty around us.

The welcome surprise is that the more you tame, the more you realize that your day-to-day activities become more manageable, and the more you are motivated to organize. It's like learning you are running a marathon with 10-pound weights strapped on your ankles and shaving minutes off your time when you drop them. You can finally take a breath. Besides lifting a heavy burden, the benefits of eliminating clutter will surprise you. Focus brings inner peace, calmness, and enthusiasm for the days ahead. You are aiming in one direction, and that alone is a relief.

Adopting a habit of decluttering paves the way for a more deliberate and fulfilling lifestyle. It allows you to allocate more time to enjoying life and relationships, both new and old, rather than constantly managing your belongings, searching for them, and cleaning them. By being ready to let go of anything that no longer serves you, you are left with only the things that you find functional or beautiful and that bring you joy. This can be a rejuvenating experience. I'm not suggesting that you get rid of everything except the furniture, but rather to keep only the items you truly cherish.

Get Rid Of:	Keepers:
Trash	Your best & finest
Similar items	Your favorites
Anything broken	Your treasures
Not used lately	
or needed	
Poor fitting items	

Simply removing clutter is a luxury because it is no longer in your sight line, reminding you that you have something to do. Tick it off your to-do list right now.

Please, please don't be intimated. Starting with one drawer or one room will give you a feeling of accomplishment when it is finished. I'll be coming out with a book and online course on decluttering soon, but an excellent first step is going through your house with a basket and throwing out trash and anything that you are absolutely sick of seeing and do not want.

If you have difficulty deciding whether to get rid of perfectly good clothes you haven't worn, remind yourself that someone will appreciate receiving them when you drop them off at a charity. The same goes for releasing a gift that doesn't suit your style and tweaks at your heartstrings.

My friend, Katie, was sentimental about getting rid of the bookcase that was her first purchase as an adult and replacing it with a piece more in line with her current style. I suggested she take a photograph, write dates and a sentiment on the back, and release it for someone else. She could go one step further and tape a second photo to the back with a meaningful note for the next owner.

I've listed some ways to bring order quickly to a few areas of your home that will have a more significant impact as you move on to larger areas.

Ideas for Organized, Clutter-Free Space

- Create a morning drawer for toiletries and cosmetics. This will save valuable a.m. time. (Details to follow.)
- Toss all the ugly, unused mugs and water bottles in the kitchen. The space you free up will amaze you.
- Sort mail the day it arrives. Shred unwanted immediately.

- Designate one spot for dirty laundry. You won't have to scour the house.
- Hang a whiteboard in your kitchen or office for only your reminders. You are more likely to accomplish it if it is written down.
- Make your bed. It looks so good that it encourages you to do more.
- Set out your clothes for the next day. Get everyone in the house to do the same. Mornings will be calmer.
- Wipe down the kitchen and put dishes in the dishwasher before bed.
- Set out coffee and cups for the morning.

Chapter 3

PERSONAL CARE

Luxury and Necessity

Few things give the feeling of luxury than being cared for. Sadly, women are typically last in this line. With everyone's busy life going non-stop, treating ourselves well is more important than ever. Self-care activities impact mental and physical health, reduce stress, and improve overall well-being. Taking care of yourself by getting enough rest and exercise can increase your energy level to take on whatever the world can throw at you— bonus points for eating healthily. Scheduling an hour on the calendar for a meeting with yourself to rejuvenate for the week ahead is an investment in your well-being.

It is hard to feel good about yourself when you're not taking care of your body. Addressing your needs through personal care can boost your self-confidence. Increased confidence will naturally occur when you practice self-care, knowing you are doing something positive for your body, mind, and spirit. Let's not forget about the effect it has on your family. When you care for yourself and meet your needs, you are better equipped to handle others in your care.

There is no denying that caring for ourselves promotes overall happiness and gives us a sense of satisfaction and fulfillment, benefiting us and everyone in our sphere. I urge you to choose one or two of these each week to pamper yourself.

- Treat yourself to a spa hour one day a week. A week rarely passes that I don't give myself a facial. It's usually more than that if I add an exfoliator, either a gentle beaded type in a tube or an electric one with a rough pad for a deeper clean. It's an excellent time to check eyebrows for stray hairs.

- Have a mani/pedi night every few weeks. Be sure you have the tools to make it easier and finish with a professional look. You can Google DIY for step-by-step instructions for giving yourself a mani-pedi at home. If you're in the mood to be pampered, visit a salon. Touch-ups between visits will be a breeze when you take your favorite polish with you.

Tip —
I take my preferred polish when I get a pro mani/pedi every few weeks. I'm always working on projects and hands need constant attention. When the inevitable chip appears, I have matching polish to touch up. Your polish will always look fresh.

- Wear cashmere socks to bed, especially for those with cold feet. Rub a few drops of foot cream to wake up to soft skin in the morning, plus it will preserve your pedicure for a longer time.

- Take a warm shower or bath with the lights dim and candles burning. This is a good time to shave your legs. A warm shower signals my body that it's time for bed, and I fall asleep faster when I do. Set the candle on a stable surface, and please remember to extinguish the candles before leaving the bathroom.

- Make time at night to thoroughly wash your face twice. Dirt and grime get moved around on your face with only one washing. Oil and dirt can enlarge your pores, and no one wants that. You may have a good complexion now, which will last much longer with some care. Use a good cleanser made for the face, and that won't dry the skin. This is the time to spend a bit more on quality products.

- Make a healthy body scrub. This is a quick and easy recipe for sugar scrub, but don't use it on your face. It is way too rough for delicate skin.

Recipe for sugar scrub for the body

3 teaspoons of olive, coconut or almond oil
1 cup of granulated sugar
a few drops of your favorite essential oil

Mix well and store in a pretty jar with a top.

- Apply a toner to level the PH on your skin. Often, this step is skipped by thinking that it is unnecessary. Balanced PH skin supports forming a healthy barrier to keep moisture and harmful bacteria out. Smoothing it on with clean fingers or a cotton pad only takes a moment. The cotton pad absorbs more than it should and wastes the toner, in my opinion.

- Since the skin around your eyes is the most delicate, use a lighter moisturizer made for this sensitive area. Regular moisturizers may be sufficient, but the more lightweight eye cream is formulated to slow down the signs of aging. It's worth the money.

- Never, ever go to bed without washing off your makeup. This includes the mascara flakes.

- Treat yourself with a leave-in overnight conditioner every few weeks to add body and manageability to your hair. It will repair damage and help you regain the luster you once had.

- Keep makeup and hairbrushes clean using baby shampoo. Your brush and comb can't do their job if they are not clean, and you don't want all that dirt and product back onto your hair. Fill your sink with warm water, add a capful of baby shampoo, and soak brushes and combs for a few minutes. Use an old toothbrush to scrub clean. A few drops of hydrogen peroxide kill any bacteria and germs.

- Exfoliate your skin once or twice a week. Your skin is the largest organ in your body and needs care to age gracefully. Besides being healthy, exfoliating regularly eliminates dry, dead skin and gives your body a lovely glow. You can always appreciate the benefit of a good skincare regime.

- Choose a scent for your signature perfume. A signature scent defines who you are. It can give others around you a sense of familiarity when they smell it. I love the summer, so it stands to reason that I choose Bobby Brown's Beach cologne for the warm months. It reminds me of summers at the neighborhood pool and the East Coast beaches as a kid. I choose a heavier scent called Mousse de Chené (oak moss) in the winter.

- Eat with awareness. I'm not here to preach about eating healthy. We all know that we should, but I am reminding you to be aware of the foods you eat and how you consume them. Are you gulping food down, or are you enjoying every bite? I love good food as much as the next woman and can eat a reasonable amount, truth be told. Mindless eating is the enemy. More calories are consumed, poor choices are made, and ultimately, we grapple with the guilty feeling. Eating with awareness helps us avoid overeating and notice which foods give us good or bad feelings. Eating the right kinds and amounts of food is crucial to our well-being.

- Avoid sugar as much as possible. Besides gaining weight and high blood pressure, sugar causes inflammation that damages your immune system and can lead to many issues, the least of which is heart disease. Sugar could be causing that blotchy red complexion you're seeing.

- Set your alarm ten minutes early so you can do your hair and makeup. It gives you more confidence and increases productivity when you look bright-eyed and bushy-tailed. I work from home and still spend ten minutes to up my game.

If you are not in the habit of doing this, be prepared for the bounce it adds to your step.

- Simplify your makeup routine. Whether you use a little or a lot of makeup, gather it in one spot to make your life easier. If your cosmetics and brushes have seen better days, go out today and buy new ones. Loose eye shadow dusting your vanity or a brush with bristles missing is frustrating and no way to start the day.

- A makeup sponge will smooth concealer and foundation on correctly and fast. If your foundation includes SPF, so much the better. Give your eyes the pop they deserve with a light application of a complimentary shadow or liner and blend. Don't forget the brows. They are the most important feature since they are so expressive. Give them a little love.

- As for lashes, the best I've found for mascara, and believe me when I say I have tried them all, is any of L'Oreal's. I like two coats with a small brush in between to separate them—finally, a sweep of blush on the cheeks. Use the powder left on the brush with a swipe on your forehead, nose, and chin. This is where the sun would color if you didn't wear SPF like a good girl. Find a quick makeup routine here on the Loverly Grey blog for an everyday makeup tutorial.

- Apply SPF to all exposed skin daily. My husband's surgeon at Johns Hopkins Hospital said that 1 in 4 people will get skin cancer. We know that using SPF on faces combats aging and the importance of spending time outside on a sunny day, but we forget about our arms and hands while driving.

- Schedule a regular annual health check. Skipping or stretching between appointments is easy when you have no symptoms and feel good. Get this on your calendar every year to detect early problems and limit your risk of diseases later on, not to mention increasing your lifespan!

- Create your happy playlist. Lift your mood with the sounds that you love.

- Subscribe to your favorite magazine. Pencil in time on the day it arrives to delight in it. Add your favorite beverage and indulge.

*You define your own life. Don't
let other people write your script.*

~ Oprah Winfrey

Chapter 4

Creating Your Space

Finding Luxury Everywhere

Every room in your home is fair game for adding little touches to elevate your life in a big way. Each small addition of fresh decor makes your home a peaceful retreat, whether a bouquet on your nightstand or new throw pillows on the couch. The unique touches only you can add create the best life for you and your family. It's these special touches that make a life that's genuinely yours.

Bath

Consider your bathroom a private sanctuary and a place to disconnect. You start and finish your day in that room. Close the door, and it becomes your place of solitude where you can relax and unwind from the day or get your day off on the right foot. Adding small touches that speak to your personality and convenience makes it unique and personal and a place you like to be for a bit of solitude.

- Get organized with a morning drawer in your bathroom with everything you need. If you carry a cosmetic bag, consider buying an additional set for the drawer rather than relying on your travel kit. Having it all at your fingertips will boost your mood, calm your nerves, and get you out of the door on time. If you are working from home, take a few minutes to brush on blush and lipstick to set your mood, boost your productivity, and be Zoom-ready.

- Get an organizer tray to straighten up your bathroom counter. Think of this as adding accessories to an outfit. Every day is more excellent when your vanity is beautiful and everything for the day is within reach. I keep my favorite earrings, bracelet, and watch in a small dish, a gift from my niece that says XOXO, reminding me of her daily. My cologne rests on a scalloped tray from my sister for a last-minute spritz.

- Set out perfumed soap. Research points to people expressing better moods and positive emotions when exposed to scents they like. Studies have also shown that smelling attractive perfumes can reduce stress and lower your heart rate. Be sure to hit the guest bath, too.

- Buy fluffy cotton towels that absorb water and feel good against your skin. This is where you want to spend a bit more on good fabric. Some towels blend synthetic and cotton, and the water gets pushed around rather than absorbed, so be sure to feel them and inspect the tag. If you want to step it up, make them monogrammed for a few extra dollars. This is also your chance to banish the old, ratty towels to the animal shelter to comfort the dogs and kitties.

- Surround your bathtub with lovely, scented candles and products that make you feel special. Using coconut wax, beeswax, or soy wax instead of paraffin is recommended for slower, longer-lasting burning and aroma.

- Sort supplies in your linen closet into baskets or trays for easy access. It is easier to pull out the tray to see the entire stock. You are likelier to use the good stuff when you open the door to find an attractive, convenient display. Toss out the things you no longer need. You know full well there are products shoved to the back that have no business being there.

- Change the shower curtain, liner, and mat. This simple change freshens the entire room. Make the mat plush to step out of the shower. The liner should be changed every six months anyway. You can bleach the devil out of that thing, and it's never good enough.

- Fold your towels like a spa. Neatly stacked towels look and fit better wherever they are stored. This website will show you step-by-step instructions to fold them in four different ways for your style. https://bit.ly/3NQc462 It only takes a minute or two to get the hang of it.

- Install decorator robe hooks. Get those bulky robes off the back of your chairs and stash them where they belong with stylish hooks. It's one more way to add a special touch to a room you use daily.

- Place a bath tray across your tub. It's the perfect place to hold a candle, book, or even your laptop to stream your favorite show while relaxing. Be sure to lock the door to keep interlopers out......at least temporarily.

- Change your shower head. If you love the idea of warm summer rain, adding a rainfall shower head should relax you just thinking about the soothing drops dancing gently around you. Close your eyes, and you'll think you got caught in a sudden drizzle. If you can't change it, clean it. Fill a sandwich bag with distilled white vinegar and fasten it around the shower head. It will sparkle after 24 hours.

- Hang artwork. Although you wouldn't want to hang a piece of irreplaceable art in the bath, adding minor pieces might be an option. Who knows? It might inspire you at the start of your day.

Tip —
Consider an inspirational quote that has relevance for you to begin and end your day. Find them framed and printed on sturdy backing for humid environments.

- Add safety and storage. A shower stool will add a safety measure on mornings when you feel wobbly and convenient storage for often used products.

- Hang eucalyptus in the shower. Loop a bundle of this mood-boosting plant over your shower head to increase energy and relieve stress and anxiety. The shower steam activates the aroma. I love their deep green color and sculpted leaves.

Indoor plants
don't just look good;
they positively impact our
moods and emotions.

- Replace drawer pulls. Throw in a set of new handles, and the room will sparkle. Opt for a show-stopping handle. Consider changing the towel bars and toilet paper holder to match while shopping.

- Roll a rolling pin over the leaves to release the scent, tie the stems together, and throw them over the shower head.

- Paint your cabinets. If your cabinets need a facelift and you feel energetic, a fresh coat of paint will do wonders. It is not as complicated as you might think, and you have a new look at the cost of a quart of paint. There are a few steps to follow, particularly priming first, to give you a finished look you'd be proud to show. Google is your friend.

- Hang a plant or place one on the vanity. Plants are aesthetically pleasing in bathrooms and make any spot fresh and inviting. They naturally absorb toxins and bacteria. Simply adding a touch of greenery is uplifting to any room. Choose one conducive to the amount of sunlight streaming through the window.

- Paint your walls a calming color. According to Houzz, some of the most relaxed-feeling colors are powder blue, spring green, and quiet violet. Google "calming colors for bathrooms," and choose your favorite soothing tones.

Your bedroom should
be a place of comfort
reserved for times of
quiet revitalizing sleep
and romantic encounters.

Bedroom

A calm and quiet bedroom is a must. This is where you retreat from the day's activities, however busy and chaotic, to your private oasis to relax and rejuvenate for the next day. A quiet room to gather your thoughts improves concentration and productivity. Besides getting a good night's sleep in an orderly bedroom, it has been shown to relieve stress and benefit your immune function and mental health.

- Sip chamomile tea in a fancy cup before retiring. You'll have sweet dreams with a relaxing cuppa before pulling the covers over your head. It has a mild sedative reaction and helps to induce sleep. Drink a cup about 45 minutes before you go to bed.

- Ditch the electronics. Seriously. Turn off your computer, iPad, TV, and phone about an hour before bed to wind down. Find something soothing like listening to music or reading to prepare for sleep.

- Wear your best stuff every day. There is no point in depriving yourself of the enjoyment of your clothes and accessories. Feeling good in your outfits gives you confidence; looking and feeling good will likely improve your performance and self-esteem. Dress for success, as they say.

- Add a photograph that makes you happy by your bedside. What better way to see someone you love than the last thing before sleep and the first after rising? Although much older now, I have a favorite of my son while in kindergarten. My heart swells every time I look at it several times a day.

- Reorganize your closet like a boutique. It makes getting dressed more fun. On the practical side, organizing makes it easier to find clothes and get dressed and allows for quickly assembling combinations that may not have come to mind. Finally, when the closet is organized, clothes stay pressed and neat. Pretty inexpensive boxes are easy to find, sort, and manage accessories for simple access. Velvety hangers are sold reasonably priced in most stores and are excellent for keeping clothes neat and pressed.

- Wear beautiful loungewear and pajamas every night. You deserve to relax in lovely, comfortable garments. Changing into pajamas signals your brain that it is time to wind down for the day. It is different from changing into after-work sweats when you arrive home to hopping into bed with those same sweats. Wearing loungewear lets you dash out for a quick errand without fuss if you must.

- Refresh your pillows. Stop punching your pillows to get them right for slumber. Pillows should be replaced every few years when they are past their peak performance. Besides, they collect allergens, dust mites, and mold over the years. Spend a little more and get a contoured one for neck support, and you might wake up with fewer aches and pains.

- Slide into new cotton bed linens. According to the National Sleep Foundation, neutral tones such as grey, blue, charcoal, and white are the best for a calming and restful environment. For softness, luxury hotels outfit their beds with 300TC or 400TC (thread count). Cotton, linen, and bamboo fabrics are the best for "hot" sleepers. Cotton is 100% hypoallergenic for those suffering from allergies. I know this isn't for everyone, but I love ironing my sheets with a spray of magic sizing to crisper them. It only takes a few minutes and feels and smells so good when I slide in at the end of a long day. It reminds me of the days that my mother hung the flapping sheets outside on the clothesline.

- Tuck lavender sachets under your pillow and in your drawers. Under your pillow, it is a stress reliever and gives you a better chance for restful sleep. It simply smells lovely In your dresser drawers. Sachets are easy to make. You can buy small amounts of lavender in stores like Whole Foods and herb farms if they are nearby. Larger quantities can be ordered from Amazon. Fill a drawstring jewelry or organza bag you have been saving with lavender and store it in the corner of your drawers. If the scent wanes briefly, rub the bag between both palms to refresh.

- Spritz your favorite scent on your pillow. If lavender is not your thing, choose an essential oil you prefer. The sweet smell relaxes and makes it easier to fall asleep. Make your own spray with 20 drops of your chosen oil, a 1:1 water ratio, and witch hazel, and store it in a glass spray bottle.

- Create a reading nook. You deserve time to slow down and recharge for your busy life. Choose a chair (move it from another room if you have to) that you can sink in while reading your favorite novel or your newly delivered favorite magazine. Accessorize with a plush throw to cuddle in the winter months, a standalone reading lamp to adjust the lighting even if it is located by a window, and a side table to keep the beverage of your choice close by. If it is not near a bookshelf, add a basket to hold your stash of books, greenery of some sort, and a pillow for comfort and color. Bonus points if you can rustle up a place to rest your weary feet. Whatever design you create, make it yours and yours alone for solitude.

- Get a good reading light. I love the convenience of electronic reading, but still love the feel of a hardback book. Reading a page-turner without squinting to see the print is a beautiful way to fall asleep without straining your eyes. A good reading light should be about 450 lumens to provide enough light but not disturb the sleep cycle. I have a rechargeable. adjustable clip-on light when the bedside lamp is insufficient. I also have a smaller one that clips onto my book.

- Make your bed every morning. Keeping your room neat and uncluttered gives a sense of pride and starts the morning on a good note. Admiral William McRaven's 2014 commencement speech at the University of Texas at Austin on the importance of making your bed every day is truly inspiring. He says that by doing so, you have accomplished the day's first task, which will encourage you to achieve another and another. This is only one of the ten life lessons he learned "to help you on your way to find a better world. Find it here: https://bit.ly/3PIWRFk. You won't regret listening to him.

- Get a lap desk to prop books and hold your nighttime tea. I've always had difficulty sipping tea and holding my book open to my reading page while lying in bed. I mentioned before how much I like a hardback book. I've had more than one cup of liquid spill over me before I became a convert.

- Dab on perfume at night. Like most appealing scents, wearing perfume to bed is relaxing. You can lightly spritz your pillow for the same effect.

- Take a nap at least one weekend day each week. Naps are underrated, and I highly recommend them. One hour or so of sleep to feel rejuvenated, and I can take on the world.

- Savor the smoothness of a dark chocolate truffle for no good reason. Treat yourself to these extraordinary confections now and then. They are especially good with a glass of Pinot Noir.

- Keep a journal. Journaling doesn't have to be time-consuming. Just five minutes a day can help you process your emotions. You can start a gratitude or inspiring quotes journal. Here's one to get you started.

I don't have to chase extraordinary moments to find happiness. It's right in front of me if I'm paying attention and practicing gratitude.
~Brené Brown

My sentiments exactly!

Kitchen

Without a doubt, the kitchen is the heart of the home. It is the room that I fell in love with immediately before Ollin and I were married. It wasn't perfect, and we have since made updates, but it was the space of it that caught my attention. Ollin said he watched me do a S-L-O-W 360 and knew we would buy this house. He loves to eat, and I am amused at the delight on his face when he sees the concoctions I whip up in our kitchen.

- Make French press coffee with freshly ground beans. Occasionally, I'll brew this coffee with the beans ground while the water is heating up.

- Serve up your smoothie in a beautiful glass. You're unique, and that's the only reason you need it.

- Drink from pretty cups to brighten any morning. Ditch the chipped cups and logo mugs. Special cups give coffee and tea the best flavor. Anthropology has some of my favorite designs.

- Make a homemade latte. There is no need to wish for an espresso machine. A microwave and instant espresso will do for now. See how the ladies of The Kitchen do it with instructions on their site: https://www.thekitchn.com/how-to-make-a-latte-without-an-espresso-machine-cooking-lessons-from-the-kitchn-211090

- In the summer, start the day with fresh berries; in winter, start with warm oats, a grated pear, and cinnamon; or try Steel-cut oats with a fried egg. If you want to go all out, crumble bacon and stir it. This is where I add a bit of fresh pepper, too.

- Top off your coffee with cream. The extra calories can't hold a candle to the richness of cream that adds to my morning coffee. Forget the half-and-half! I have the real thing for only a few more calories.

- Set up a coffee bar the night before. Lay out everything you need to have coffee at your fingertips, eliminating any morning decisions. My hubby likes it so much that he sets it out himself, along with the cat's breakfast and the Ninja for his morning smoothie.

- Display and serve sugar cubes for hot drinks. This is for no other reason than they look lovely in a pretty bowl.

- Make cold brew. It's easier to make than you think. https://bit.ly/46xyY9L

- Use your good wine glasses for yourself. Thin glasses help to underscore the acidity and color of the wine, and it always tastes better. There is a psychological aspect adding elegance to your wine-tasting experience.

- Ask Alexa for her choice of Italian music. Schedule an hour or so, pop open a bottle of red wine, slip on your favorite apron, and whip up your best home-cooked meal (assuming you love to cook.) I enjoy doing this on a Saturday evening when I have the time without neglecting work-related responsibilities that need attention.

- Enhance the taste with a pepper grinder. The flavor and texture will always be superior to the pre-ground stuff. I like the coarse texture because the pieces are large enough to taste.

- Stock up on a variety of flavored and finishing salts. They add a zip and interest to your favorite recipes.

- Set out cloth napkins for meals. Whether eating before a fully set table or in front of the TV for dinner, cloth napkins elevate any dining experience.

- Keep a stocked pantry. At a moment's notice, I know I can whip up a meal for dinner or company without dashing out to the store. We eat a lot of salads, so I add spring mix from a hydroponic farm nearby year-round to my weekly shopping list. My kitchen is rarely without the following:

Pantry Essentials

Pantry
- mushrooms
- plum tomatoes
- tiny, canned potatoes
- black and green olives
- olive oil
- chicken, beef, and vegetable stock
- cornbread
- peppercorns
- red pepper flakes
- capers
- coarse salt
- pasta
- nuts
- crackers
- coffee/tea
- chocolate covered candy
- Tuna in olive oil
- anchovies
- mustard
- black beans
- artichokes

Fridge
- green peppers (longer shelf life than others)
- eggs
- spring salad mix
- olives
- artichokes
- cornichons or sweet pickles
- blueberries
- avocados *
- strawberries **
- cream
- dried herbs
- peppered salami
- cheese
- lemon & lime juice
- garlic

Freezer
- cut up frozen chicken
- grass-fed ground beef
- Salmon filets
- shrimp

Drinks
- sparkling water
- still water
- wine
- beer
- aperitif of some sort
- vodka (optional)
- Aperol (optional) (See recipe below.)

- tonic water
- club soda
- split of champagne

*Wrap avocados in tin foil and store them in the refrigerator or a pitcher of water to keep them from ripening too quickly. I know. I was surprised, too. They will keep for 6-7 days.
** Strawberries will keep longer if you add a folded paper towel to the length of the plastic container and store it upside down.

- Run a runner. Place a patterned runner in front of the sink to spice things up. Runners usually come in 7, 10, and 12-foot lengths. Target and Wayfair have inexpensive ones for as little as $45. Ruggables brand is a bit more pricey but washable. If you're like me, this is a smart buy, as I'm a little sloppy with the cooking.

- Refresh your hardware. There are beautiful cabinet handles priced reasonably online. It's a cost-effective way to brighten up the kitchen. All you will need is a screwdriver and 30 minutes of your time.

- Stock a few artisan oils and sauces. Nothing perks up the taste of a vinaigrette like premium olive oil. You can definitely taste the difference. We love truffle oil and the hot sauce that raises scrambled eggs to new heights.

- Eat Irish butter. It tastes better than American butter due to its higher fat content and lower water count. Cows in Ireland are primarily grass-fed, and the carotene gives butter its rich yellow color.

- Grow fresh herbs. Besides the scrumptious taste, herbs add a dash of color, a lovely fragrance, and simple beauty to your home. You'll have fresh herbs for a tastier option than dried spices. I rub my hands through the lavender and rosemary in our yard every chance I have. Our mint adds a refreshing zip to tea. I love dashing out to the back to snip a few basil leaves for the salads I prepare for most dinners, especially in the summer. I would grow it inside in the garden window if I could keep our cat, Leonard, from eating it in the middle of the night. Basil tends to upset his sensitive constitution.

- Make fresh salad dressing. Homemade dressing is the healthier option to avoid saturated fats, extra sodium, and sugar in most store-bought brands. It's up-to-the-minute fresher, too. See my recipes for salad and dressing that follow.

- Shop at farmer's markets. You'll help the local economy, and fruits and vegetables will last longer and taste better than most supermarkets without adding sauces or butter.

- Play uplifting music wherever you are working. I go old school when cooking dinner on Friday nights with Glen Campbell songs on Alexa. It doesn't feel like work when I add a glass of my favorite chardonnay. When Ollin hears the music coming from the kitchen, he knows it's time to appear for a dance around the kitchen between flipping burgers. Try an Aperol Spritz if wine isn't your thing. The simple recipe is on page 59.

Connie's Homemade Vinaigrette

One-half cup extra virgin olive oil,
Three tablespoons of balsamic vinegar *
a pinch of salt
a dash of Italian spices

*You can substitute any vinegar and fresh herbs if you have them. Lately, I've been adding strawberry-infused balsamic vinegar and freshly chopped basil from the garden.

Connie's Mediterranean Salad

a handful of spring mix
a handful of chopped romaine lettuce
Six tiny tomatoes halved
One-half chopped cucumber quartered
Three artichoke hearts, chopped in half
Six black olives
1/2 avocado, chopped
Six oz. diced chicken breast or whole shrimp
Three or four leaves of chopped basil
a pinch of salt

Layer the ingredients in a large bowl in the order given. Add the vinaigrette recipe below according to taste. Serve with fresh bread with fresh bread and a glass of white Sancerre. Serves one.

If it doesn't add to your life, let it go.

Living Room

Nowadays, the trend is to merge kitchens, dining areas, and living rooms into a single space rather than having separate rooms for each activity. However, the living room remains the most important place where people spend time together, engage in conversations, and create cherished memories. Our living room is an eclectic mix with a cushy leather couch to sink into and a well-loved coffee table to prop our feet to read. Our cats, Leonard and Loretta, sleep lazily above on their fleece blankets on the back of the couch.

- Style your living room coffee table. Consider varying heights for balance and interest. Candles do the trick. Add a stack of vintage or oversized coffee table books, a brass figurine, and a decorator tray. You can add texture here with a woven tray. If you are a collector, display one or two things you love. Of course, fresh flowers and greenery are always lovely. Leave room for drinks. You get the idea. Google "how to" or Pinterest for a million ideas, then shop your home for the items. Thrift shops are great for finding wooden bowls, candle sticks, and such.

- Plump a few textured pillows. Textures of any kind add a graceful and luxurious feel to any room. Pillows, chunky throws, sisal rugs, and baskets are all intelligent choices to spice up the room. If you're thinking of new furniture pieces, velvet/velour, leather, wood grain, metal, mohair, or grass cloth, it will shake it up. A splash of color or print doesn't hurt. Be brave!

- Include metal accent pieces. Add a dash of character, personality, and sophistication to a space with any metal-like details. They add depth and dimension. Feel free to mix the metals, adding a luxurious look to the room. If you are going to go that route, be sure the like metals are similar in tone, or it looks off.

- Will you choose Warm or Cool? Metals like gold and copper add warmth and coziness to the room, while aluminum and stainless steel are cool.

- Decorate with mirrors and vintage picture frames. Mirrors bounce light, maximizing natural light, and ornate picture frames add interest. They brighten and open a small room by placing the mirror near a window. A wall gallery, including a mirror, makes quite an impact.

- Cover your couch with a linen throw. Linen is considered a luxury fabric with a nice bit of texture. Try the Linen Locker for large throws to cover and add style to otherwise shabby seating. They come in a variety of colors. They are a fresh way to "summerize" your home during the warm months. FYI: If the current fabric on your couch is pilling (some synthetic fabrics do that), buy an inexpensive fabric shaver (Joann Fabrics or

Amazon) and shave the pills away. Easy-peasy. It's suitable for sweaters, too.

- Create a home bar. Nothing says chic like a home bar. Pinterest has many ideas, from a rolling cart to a repurposed cabinet or bookshelf—even a piano.

- Add mood lighting. Think battery-operated wall sconces, rechargeable LED strips, or under-counter lights to add a bit of drama to any room.

- Consider black and white wall art that adds sophistication. It just feels more expensive.

- Install an oversized art piece. Large pieces over the couch or leaning on an otherwise bare wall lend themselves to lavishness. It adds drama and focus and makes a lasting style impression in a large or small room. Think texture.

- Cover books with wrapping paper. Dress up uninteresting books for display with wrapping paper in designs and colors that complement your decor. Cover any old book. It works with paperbacks, too. Use them for stacking or adding height to a smaller decorator piece. I've seen large books stacked high enough for a small side table.

Aperol Spritz

Aperol, Prosecco, Club Soda, Orange Slice

This is my favorite mixed drink and is shamefully easy to make. It brings back beautiful images of a trip to Luxembourg several years ago to visit my friends Brian and Jeni, who moved from the East Coast. We sampled tasty chocolates in Belgium between spritzes and toured the Taittinger champagne cellars in France. Sipping it brings back lovely memories of that "Summer of Fun," as Jeni calls it.

———

Aperol is a zesty orange aperitif. You will find it near the liqueurs at a liquor store. Prosecco is an Italian sparkling wine; a dry one is suggested so it doesn't turn too sweet—club soda for the fizz and a fresh orange slice for the garnish. Add ice, and you're done.

Fill your favorite wine glass with ice, pour the Aperol followed by Prosecco, a splash of club soda, and don't forget the orange slice. You can skip the orange slice, but I wouldn't. It's like giving a birthday present without a bow. The details count. The ratio is 1:1 of Aperol and Prosecco with a splash of club soda. Add more club soda if you want less alcohol. Aperol's slightly bitter taste isn't for everyone but can be altered with more Prosecco.

Dining Room

In some homes, dining room tables serve as a catch-all for everything that doesn't have a specific resting place, so it is rarely used for its intended purpose — meals and entertaining guests. There are just the two of us in our house, so we don't have meals there, but I love dinner parties at our 1800s Scottish antique table. The well-worn leg at the head of the table, where we presume the man of the house sat all those years ago, is quite a conversation starter.

- Light it up. If the room lacks light, set a table lamp or two on a side buffet or shelf to add to it. No outlet nearby? Get a battery-operated lamp. You can create any mood you'd like by switching them on or off.

- Snap on a new outlet. If you live in an older house with those ugly outlet covers, an immediate upgrade is a 1-Gang Decorator Style Wall Plate. This modern-style outlet plate gives outlets and light switch plates a new look. Amazon had it the last time I looked.

- Clear the clutter. Many people use their dining room table for everything other than eating. Clear everything except an eye-catching centerpiece, such as a large dough bowl with fake artichokes or pears or a large hurricane glass with a fat candle. Maybe a beautiful tapestry runner?

60

- Add a touch of color. Paint is inexpensive, so painting your walls only takes some elbow grease. I know, I know, it's tedious, but it's worth the effort when you stand back and admire your handiwork. It transforms the dining room, or any room for that matter. Better Homes & Gardens is already coming in hot on the 2024 Colors of the Year, as they do every year. If you're itching to be on trend, you have a wide range from earthy tones of terra cotta and green to bold ones like cracked pepper. Websites like <u>Veranda.com</u> offer lists of the best colors for different rooms. Go for it! The choice is yours.

- Mat your photos. Matting gives an immediate high-end feel to your photographs. Thicker mats in black frames, say two inches or so, are inexpensive and provide posh pictures or artwork. Larger frames are a statement piece. You can find reasonably priced original artwork on Etsy. I love the look of a 5x7 or smaller photograph in an oversized mat and frame. (Hobby Lobby and Michaels for ready-made.)

- Crank up some tunes. Music provides the perfect backdrop for the ambiance you want to create. Remember to keep the volume to a level for people to converse normally.

- Add a rug. According to Home Edit, a dining room rug must be at least 18-24" longer than all sides of your table. When in doubt, err on the side of too big.

- Create a cactus garden. Find a large glass bowl or several smaller ones the same size, fill the bottom with pebbles, and arrange a variety of plastic cactuses over the stones. They look so natural. Fill the bowl to mid-level with water for a garden you don't have to tend.

- Bring out the good silverware and china. This is likely not the first time you've heard this suggestion, but it is worth mentioning again. Who better to treat with style than you and your loved ones?

- Add candles to the table for their aesthetic and emotional value. A single candle can bring down the stress level and have a positive emotional impact. The flattering light is a bonus!

Laundry

Very few people consider anything having to do with laundry a luxury, but we must do it whether we like it or not. While having the inhabitants of your home pick up their socks and drop them in the laundry basket occasionally would send you waltzing into the next room, it's not going to happen. You'll have to take control of your mood when rescuing the stray sock and
t-shirt. These ideas may not be your idea of luxury, but they will surely make your life easier and brighter. Most of all, a well-organized laundry will save time and stress.

- Paint it a bright color. Splash the walls with a bold color to lift your spirits, especially if you find yourself camping out there. If your laundry is in the corner of a dingy basement, you can still create a happy place by blocking it with paint, a folding table, and an area rug to brighten it.

- Roll in an oversized cart or table. Add one if your laundry room doesn't have a folding counter. Folding and sorting are much easier when you have space to spread out. It's easier on your back if it accommodates standing. It also keeps unfolded clothes from finding their way into other rooms.

- Unfold a drying rack. Draping clothes over the rack is less hassle than hanging everything or if you can't string a line. Fold it away when not in use.

- Hang your ironing board. Install two fancy coat hooks a few inches apart, high enough to lift the board above the baseboard. This keeps it out of the way until you need it, yet it is easy to set up and put away. For a few dollars, buy a new cover that matches the paint and accessories you will add.

- Hang an over-the-door shelf. Keep laundry and cleaning supplies handy, not taking up valuable shelf space.

- Add a mirror to brighten the space. Brighten up the room with bouncing light. See living room suggestions for ideas.

- Hang artwork. A laundry room is an excellent place to add life using artwork or inspiring quotes.

- Use a few drops of essential oil in your washing machine to make your clothes smell heavenly. Try bergamot or basil for extra energy.

- Decant the products you use most often. Visit thrift shops for containers with lids. If you don't want to buy them, save the bigger plastic jars that some snacks come in. Go the extra mile with a can of spray paint and cover the top to match the decor.

Add a hand-lettered chalk label, and voila, you're in business.

- Add a put-away basket. This keeps the folded clothes ready to go to their respective rooms. Be sure to label it clearly so that the person you designate to put it away will not have an excuse to complete the job.

- Add some greenery. Give the room some warmth with a plant that doesn't require a lot of light and maintenance. The Snake, Spyder, Pathos, Lucky Bamboo. and Fern are good choices. If all else fails, an artificial plant will do.

Workplace

Whether you work from home or in an office, these ideas will make your day brighter. Take the time to make it a special place that you enjoy coming to. You'll notice a spike in your productivity if it is organized and beautiful.

- Clean and organize your desk/table. Your productivity will get a boost.

- Add a desk mat. It looks fresh, will keep your keyboard from sliding, and offers an excellent writing surface.

- Keep wipes handy to clean your computer screen and keyboard. You won't misread a crucial word hidden behind smudge marks.

- Change your lock screen and wallpaper to a color or image that inspires and gives you happiness.

- Order personalized stationery or notecards. Your correspondence will be extra special to the receiver.

- Keep stamps on hand. I buy them in bulk from the post office because I'm all about sending cards and handwritten notes.

- Purchase a good ballpoint or fountain pen. It is a great sensual experience to write on fine paper with a good pen. Besides looking stylish, they lend a touch of sophistication. It just feels good.

- Dress up your books. Take the jacket off a few old books you have lying around and cover them with the large artistic sheets of wrapping paper you see hanging in stationery stores to complement your decor. Heavy brown paper also looks great when you bind three books with heavy brown twine or ribbon. (Also suggested for the dining room.)

- Store sealing wax in your stationery box to add a touch of class to your notes and cards. I know this might be over the top, but I love to melt gold wax onto the envelope and stamp it with a "P" to finish it. Your notes will be memorable because no one else is doing it.

- Lighten your mood with accessories. Fun magnets, colorful notepads, folders, and pushpins add extra personality, particularly if you are assigned to a cube.

- Lay a rug to define the space. If you are lucky enough to have an office in your company's building or a home office, decorate it like any other area. A rug adds personality, visual interest, and texture. Although carpets don't absorb sound completely, they will help to minimize it. Buy a rug at least two feet larger than your desk and large enough that all chairs rest easily on it.

- Paint the walls in your home office a color that makes you happy. This idea assumes you have a say in your paint selection. Different colors will affect your mood, especially if you have no windows, so pick one that lifts it. Your office color will help you transition from work to home, and finding motivation some days is hard.

- Hang a gallery wall with your favorite art. Mix art with your favorite photographs for an inspiring pick-me-up every time you glance at it. Add photos of your family to remind you of the reason you work so hard every day.

- Keep duplicates of printer ink and paper. You won't run out of them or be stuck waiting for your Amazon order to arrive.

- Always, always add greenery. I can't say that enough.

- And for heaven's sake, get a comfortable office chair. You deserve this much comfort for the amount of time you spend in it.

Car

So here you are, dressed to the nines, stepping into a filthy car scattered with old receipts, the random carry-out straw wrapper, and half-full plastic water bottles rolling around on the floor. Don't be that person.

Flashback to how good it felt riding in your new, fresh-smelling car. It doesn't matter whether it is a Mercedes or a Mazda; something is uplifting about a spit-shined car. Give these few ideas a try to revive that new car feeling.

- Use disinfectant wipes in your car to wipe off the dash while waiting in the bank or pharmacy drive-in line. It will give you a social media break and a shine simultaneously.

- Shake off your shoes before getting in. It's easier than shaking out the mats.

- Always take everything that doesn't belong in the car when you get to the office or home. It will save you time later, and cleaning your vehicle won't be as much of a chore.

- Keep a plastic bag attached to the back seat pocket. Empty it every time you stop for gas. Schedule a regular inside and out cleaning at the car wash at least every six months and between your cleanings. It forces you to clean out the clutter if you are not inclined to follow the "take everything with you" suggestion.

- Add a new air freshener with each cleaning. I switch between beachy scents in the summer and leather in the cooler months. Pop it under the floor mat to store it out of the way.

Outside

Ollin and I have spent endless hours and sweat making our home an oasis inside and out. We drive past our house, saying to one another, "Who lives there? They must love their home." A spacious front porch with two rocking chairs sits in front of our home, where we enjoy our morning coffee and admire the neighborhood behind the blue hydrangeas during summer mornings.

- Paint your front door black. Homes and Gardens says a black door can add $ 6,500 more to the value of your home. Who knew? Our door is navy blue on a white brick house, and I love it, but I must admit I secretly want that Southern Robin's egg blue.

- Change the wreath on your door seasonally. Organize them in labeled trash bags to keep them fresh and easy to hang in a closet or attic. I buy them off-season and can expect at least a 50% discount.

- Create an outdoor conversation space in your yard. The pieces don't need to be expensive; arrange a defined area to enjoy. Wayfair has some inexpensive, fun outdoor seating and decor that is up to the task.

- Position your chairs around a cocktail table to create a conversation area. Lay an outdoor rug to define the space.

- Style the table with a runner and a few knick knacks like a metal tray or a plant in a lovely planter. Add height with a book or two, a candle atop, a glassware piece, and a wine cooler or ice bucket.

- Spray paint random thrift store chairs a single color for a cohesive look. They will coordinate easily with their surroundings.

- Add outdoor pillows. Add color and texture for interest.

- Hang a non-working chandelier in a tree, wrap trailing vines around it, or use battery-powered lighting for ambiance. Finish the look by wrapping lights around the tree trunk.

- Plant flowering perennials. You'll have fresh colors every year without the extra labor. Water them well after planting and mulch around them to retain moisture. Water every day during the first week unless plenty of rain falls during any day.

- Define the patio space with a few large potted plants. The plants add interest and soften the otherwise hardscape of the patio. An intimate cafe feeling will emerge with tables and chairs and other seating. To establish a flow, you'll need to develop a pattern, i.e., the same color or size of pots.

- Add a few stepping stones. Create a walkway to "somewhere" in your yard and garden, to a fire pit, or the children's play area: river rocks, slate, fieldstone, or concrete combined with gravel. Let moss and grass grow between them.

- Hang some plants on an overhang or metal rod. Think spring rod if the plants aren't too heavy and you have two walls to attach to. Besides adding the finishing touches to an outdoor area, they will be safe from nasty weather. Be sure that they are light enough to handle the weight and get the right-sized hooks.

- Add a few poufs or garden stools as seating or side tables. Move them around for easy and accessible conversation spots. They add a homey feeling to your space; garden stools can weather the weather. They are also engaging in their shapes and colors.

- Fashion an outdoor bar cart or table. Nearly any flat surface will do. If you're handy, there are plenty of instructions online to build one. If not, pick up one of those 1950s metal tea carts you see in thrift stores and give it a pop of color with paint.

As mentioned in the Living Room section, I've seen bookshelves and other cabinets converted with a few changes. Again, Wayfair is calling. Don't overlook Pinterest for ideas.

- Tuck in a hammock and pillows under a tree in the corner of your yard for an ideal spot. How about your porch for another excellent spot? Sink into it for a relaxing afternoon of summer reading.

- Build a fire pit with a few landscaping blocks. There are easy diagrams for a simple pit design. Whether you build or buy fire pits, they will add a glow to your entertaining. It provides warmth on chilly nights and looks marvelous when surrounded by a planned seating arrangement of furniture. You'll dine casually outside more often when your yard has this focal point. S'mores always taste better around the fire.

- Light your walkway, front and back, with solar-powered lights. The obvious reason is for safety and saving money, but they add interest while serving as a guide to your door.

- Install a small fountain or birdbath water feature. Any large pot or receptacle will do. Purchase an immersible pump on Amazon, and you are in business.

- Give potted plants a finished look by scattering small stones or artificial moss on top of the soil. The stones come in all colors and sizes. This significantly impacts small trees or plants with fewer leaves near the bottom when most dirt is visible. You can't see them with a bushy plant like geraniums.

- Plant some ground cover. Plants like Lily Turf or Lavender are perfect for adding a plush look to your yard. A bonus is less to mow and care for.

Chapter 5

Entertaining Yourself & Others

Making Fun

Hosting a gathering at home has its perks. You can enjoy the comfort of your space, play your preferred music, and operate things at your own pace. What better way to share your home? I have a few ideas to encourage you to invite friends or spend time alone with your partner.

- Host a BYOB backyard wine and cheese party. Serve cheeses from around the world or assign a country. Or you could have guests bring cheese and wine from that location, plus a fun fact about the locale. If that's too much, have the wine chilled and waiting for them to arrive.

- Pack a bottle of wine, cheese, and a baguette and walk among the trees. The exercise is good, and the scenery is relaxing. Find a sweet spot for a picnic on the way.

- Rent a fancy car for the day and explore within an hour or two from home. If you've always dreamed of having an exotic car, you can scratch that itch by tracking down a company that will rent for a few days. You can up your vacation experience because why not? Consider the additional day rental insurance for your peace of mind.

- Buy the best cheap wine. Check out the wine reviews. There are plenty of good ones under $20. Some are even rated at 90 or above. <u>Food & Wine</u> is an excellent resource. My favorite is Kendall Jackson Vintner's Reserve, which hovers around that price when it is on sale. I love the oaky highlights.

- Go to a regional or university theater or symphony. Ticket prices are usually reasonable and support the local economy. Wear your best duds for the occasion.

- Splurge on expensive ice cream. Undoubtedly, the higher-priced kinds are richer, silkier, and, thus, more satisfying! Find a quiet spot and eat it all yourself.

- Get your car valeted on your next outing. Ladies, take advantage of the opportunity to wear high heels. You know, the ones you haven't worn since the lockdown? Get a charge from sweeping past the valet as you toss him the keys and a few bills before parking to ensure he's careful with your car. You'll have to tip the guy bringing it back, too. I hand the return valet the ticket and tip together and typically get better service.

- Stop by the best place in town for a drink. Order their signature cocktail or better wine.

- Get a creative hobby. Scan YouTube for ideas if you don't have one of your own. Domestika is another inexpensive online lesson site. You can have an expert in the field show you how it's done for a few dollars. Masterclass is another excellent resource with an annual subscription.

- Host a Ted Talk night. Gather your besties and watch all the talks you didn't have time for. Take 10 minutes in between to refresh drinks and discuss the topic.

- Go to art openings. This is one activity that you can do alone. If you have the time, Google the artist beforehand to help you understand the work. You never know who you might meet. At the very least, expect an exciting conversation.

- Schedule a coffee date with a friend at a swanky restaurant. Catch up on the latest goings on. Only order coffee and a decadent dessert, and plan to do it again before you part company.

- Go to the cinema that has reserved reclining seats. Reserve the best spot a few days ahead. Get the bottomless popcorn with butter. I've often watched movies by myself and love the experience.

- Go to book readings. Even small towns have local authors happy to oblige. After writing this one, I appreciate the hard work that goes into their books. Honestly, it is a labor of love.

- Google all the Happy Hours in your town. Hit one of them every Thursday, huddle with friends at a corner table, and laugh your head off.

- Catch a minor league or university baseball game. Seek out the best high school football games in the fall. You don't have to travel far, the crowds are smaller, and you can't beat the price. Pat yourself on the back for supporting the locals and the kids.

- Stroll the farmer's markets. Take in the sights of the gorgeous fruits, vegetables, and handmade goods, all lovingly created by your neighbors.

- Visit the Visitors Center. Stop by the Visitors Center in your town. I'll bet you dollars to donuts, there will be some discovery that has escaped your notice.

Connie Paradise

Chapter 6

Refreshing the Lost Luxury

Brush Up on Social Graces

Heaven knows I'm not an authority on etiquette. I can be as relaxed as the next gal in some situations, so I did check with several sources to be sure I'm not leading you astray before spouting off my thoughts on this aspect of life. Also, I must confess that I've made more than my share of faux pas over the years. Social graces refer to polite and kind behavior, including etiquette and manners, and I hear repeatedly that they have died for the most part.

Showing good manners is essential because it demonstrates respect and care towards others. More importantly, they allow us to show off our best selves to the world, help us appear more confident, and make us feel good while putting them into practice.

From my perspective, social graces are one of life's overlooked luxuries. So many seem to have flown out of the window—even the simple ones. Including social graces in your daily life means that you care about the dignity of others and treat them with the respect I am assuming we all want to receive.

Although it appears that the rude behavior phenomenon has recently sprung up around us, I'm pretty sure people have been saying this for decades, if not centuries. I say this confidently because I stumbled on a quote by Fred Astaire, a dancer extraordinaire from the 1930s. He said, "The hardest job kids face today is learning manners without seeing any." Whether or not manners and etiquette are practiced, society rules how we behave toward others.

These days, most people are hustling from one place to another in a hurry, thinking about everything but where they are in the moment. Is the new neighbor's housewarming this weekend? Did I pick up this week's dry cleaning? Has the pet turtle been fed today? With so much on their minds, it's easy to draw inward and march onward with a purpose to accomplish your tasks in the limited time you feel you have, forgetting about those around you.

I'm not going to dwell on how it happened because you probably know as well as I do that the internet had a hand in it, as does the busyness of our lives. This is no excuse, of course. There are a multitude of reasons why this disrespect is happening now. It's not mine to identify or solve for the greater good, only to manage my small corner of the world to honor other humans. Some days, it's tough though.

As incredible and life-changing as the internet is, it has moved the needle in the wrong direction in adhering to polite social norms for some. I can't believe some of the comments I read. Whenever I encounter one of the crass comments online, I feel moved to bless the person and move on. All I can think is that they must be so unhappy to use up a minute of this valuable life to be so ugly.

Tip —
Be warm and enthusiastic. Maintain an open and confident attitude.

Certainly, manners have changed over the last century and become more relaxed, but common courtesies toward people are still a general requirement in a civilized society. Our society must employ social graces to function correctly, and we are failing miserably.

Imagine how smoothly your day would go if those around you considered others. I believe most people try to do a good job and get through the day as best they can.

There are tomes written about the rules of good manners and etiquette that can't be covered here, so I'll offer a few of the more important ones. After talking with many people, I confidently say they will welcome suggestions.

- Always offer a good handshake and look the person in the eyes. It also helps if you say their name, especially if you don't know them. Like "So nice to meet you, so and so." Or "Great to see you again, so and so."

- Say Please, Thank you, May I and You're Welcome.

- Stand when shaking hands, regardless of your gender. This takes the guesswork out of a potentially awkward situation.

- Air kissing is one step above a handshake. It is your choice to make the kiss sound while gently bumping the other's cheek.

- Open doors for others. The general rule is that the first through the door holds it for the others. And yes, ladies, you can hold the door for a man—a definite yes for someone who is elderly or struggling with their arms full.

- Give genuine compliments. Sometimes, I tell women passing by how good they look in a particular color or dress style. Their face lights up when they hear it.

- Be genuinely interested in others. Listen when they speak. Ask them questions about themselves. Make eye contact when talking to someone.

- Always be punctual, but give the person you're meeting two minutes of advance notice every minute you are late. If you're running ten minutes late, inform the other party twenty minutes beforehand.

- Don't apologize profusely if you're late. If you make it a big deal, it becomes a big deal. Say, "Thank you for waiting for me." If you are chronically late, now that's another story.

- Never put your elbows on the table. Resting your forearms is acceptable.

- Discards like olive and cherry pits, bones, and tea bags go to the upper left of the plate. On that note, "how it goes in is how it comes out." If an olive pit went in with your fingers, take it out the same way. Sauces added to your plate go to the bottom right of the plate.

- Immediately put your napkin on your lap when seated in a restaurant. When dining in someone's home, please wait until the host or hostess places the napkin on their lap before you do so. Make sure the crease is always facing you.

- Place your napkin in your chair to let the wait staff know you are coming back. Pinch the center and place the napkin to the left of your plate when you finish your meal.

- Say "excuse me" when going to the restroom. No one wants you to be explicit.

- Keep your voice to a level only those at your table can hear, not the entire restaurant.

- Show people you remember significant life events. Keep a perpetual planner for birthdays and anniversaries. Have a stash of greeting cards and stamps on hand for all occasions.

- Send thank you notes or texts for a gift or kind gesture.

- Don't post pictures on the internet without permission.

- Don't leave long, rambling voicemails. Keep them brief.

- Put your phone away when you're with others. It would be best to give the people present your full attention.

- Clean up your dog's mess. Is there anything more infuriating than random piles? Attachable gadgets to hold bags on leashes are sold everywhere. No excuses! And for heaven's sake, don't let them do it in someone's yard.

- Cover your mouth when you cough or sneeze. Sneeze or cough into your shoulder or the back of your hand. Isn't this simply common sense? Plus, who wants to see a distorted face mid-sneeze?

- In most places, staying to the right when walking is acceptable and takes the guesswork out of passing. This amazes me because people sometimes try to squeeze in on the right when passing.

There are many more, but you get where I'm coming from.

Connie Paradise

Chapter 7

Being A Good Dinner and House Guest

Putting Your Best Foot Forward

When you accept an invitation to someone's house for dinner, you expect the hostess to make you feel welcome and valued. Similarly, as a guest, you must show your appreciation and kindness towards the hostess. The host and guest can have a fantastic time by adhering to these unwritten guidelines.

Many of the suggestions apply to an evening with friends or a weekend. Use your best judgment.

- Arrive a few minutes late to give your host extra time unless she is a super hostess.

- Bring a small gift. Wrap it beautifully, if you can. I've always considered the presentation part of the gift.

- Write a thank you note within a day or two of the visit.

- Toast them. Keep these toasts in your back pocket to personalize for nearly every occasion.

  "May we have more and more friends and need them less and less."

  "May good fortune precede you; love walk with you and good friends follow you."

- Always ask if you can bring anything. People usually say "no"; however, I'll get a bottle of wine or a bouquet. It is not necessary to drink the wine you bring with you. The host may have other plans.

- Offer to help. A friend complained about a visitor who made it obvious she was on vacation and did nothing to help. It ruffled some feathers.

- Ask if you should take off your shoes. That said, check your socks before leaving the house.

- Please clean up the sink in the bathroom after using it. Honestly, this is a polite thing to do wherever you use the loo. Without going into sickly details, I am appalled at how some women leave the sinks at the gym.

- Bring everything you need. Don't expect them to provide anything.

- Check with your host before accepting an invitation from someone other than the host.

- Make your bed and clean up after yourself. Ask them if they prefer you to strip the bed on your last morning. They may want to do it their way. If they say yes, put the bed cover on and place the folded sheets at the bottom. Want the Gold Star Houseguest Award? Ask them if you can make the bed with fresh linens.

  Always ask before you bring your pet. An excellent way to ask without asking is to inquire about a kennel nearby or offer to stay at a hotel. This gives your host a chance to invite the pet.

- Above all, make your visit short and sweet unless your host has begged you to stay longer.

- Don't make anyone blush. Always be clothed when leaving your room.

- Ask to approach their pet or wait until the pet comes to you. This is a good rule of thumb in a home or street. Animals are unpredictable.

- Don't expect your host to entertain you. They have probably seen the nearby museum or shopping mall a thousand times. Do a little legwork before leaving home for sights you want to see if your host offers to take you, so much the better.

- Treat them to a lovely dinner/evening out.

- Offer to pay for groceries if your host needs last-minute items or you have an extended stay. You don't have to show up at the door with grocery bags, so talk to your host beforehand to determine the best way.

- Adhere to their schedule. If breakfast is served at 7:30 a.m. on a Saturday, hop out of bed by 7:25 a.m. and make your way to the kitchen.

This is not an exhaustive list but a compilation of the ones you will likely encounter. This was an excellent refresher, and I needed clarification on a few.

Chapter 8

Ruling Money Matters

Controlling Your Finances

Another feeling not typically associated with luxury is the feeling you get when freeing yourself from the stress of out-of-control finances. Being burdened with debt is a huge stress point. It can cause increased stress levels at work, performance, and sleep disruption, not to mention mental health issues. Get your finances and your life under control with a few helpful suggestions. (This book is not financial advice or recommendations. Consult your financial advisor for information and advice.

Disposable income gives you the freedom to decide how you want to spend your money, and having the extra dollars to spend on little luxuries is extra sweet. I make a game of how I can live luxuriously for less, and sometimes, those tiny wins give me an incredible thrill. That's not to say I don't splurge or take advantage of something I've planned. Spending less doesn't mean the top-of-the-line stuff is out of your reach. It simply means spending smarter. With a bit of decluttering that I'm sure you did at the beginning of this book, you can identify and focus on what matters to you and spend your money on that.

> **Tip —**
> Pay your bills on time. This is the best way to increase your credit score and save money on insurance and loans.

Being aware of the things you buy is half the battle. When I pop in line for a Venti latte at Starbucks, there is never a shortage of people ahead of me. So, if you are one of them, is that $5.00 every five days a week worth it, or could you make your coffee at home in a to-go mug and buy down your credit card debt with an extra $100 a month? Your choice.

Another area where you can quickly lose control is the subscription realm, especially electronics. That $10 trial for the first year of Vogue turns into an auto-renewal at $35 a year. How about the Alexa music app at $4.99 a month, or would free Pandora suit your needs at the gym? That's another $60.00 a year you could pop into savings. It adds up quickly when you're not looking. I'm not suggesting that you give up everything except the necessities. Look at your expenses and be honest about the things that matter and that you actually use. Ask yourself if a low-cost alternative will do just as well. It sneaks up on you, people!

Don't get caught on the slippery slope of buying something just because it is on sale. You don't love or need it, and you wouldn't have given it a second thought, except IT'S ON SALE! Rather than buying many things you feel lukewarm about, skipping a few sale items could add up to the cost of an item you set your heart on.

- Don't spend more than you make; #1 rule.

- Buy only the things you really love. If you love them, you'll be happier with your purchase.

- Think before you buy. Before making an impulsive purchase, consider how often you'll use it to avoid post-purchase anxiety. Pause and take a deep breath. You may decide you don't need it at all.

- Create an emergency fund. This amount is at least six months of your salary. Use the money you've saved on coffees and subscriptions above to contribute to it.

- Don't spend to make yourself happy. A small shopping splurge is okay, but you must slow down if you've become obsessed.

- Calculate cost per use. Divide the item's price by the number of times you think you will wear/use it. That cashmere sweater may come out of your closet once a week and again on weekends. Three hundred dollars divided by 104 in one year equals $2.88 per wear for one year. With proper care, a high-quality cashmere garment can last for many years. (Now, that's a good buy.)

- Never shop in person or online due to boredom. Do not. I repeat, do not open your phone or laptop if you are bored. Find a good book or go for a walk.

- Create a budget for personal shopping. Set a budget for each category and pinky swear with your bestie that you won't go over it. Pay cash or limit credit card spending to only the amount you allocated for that category.

- Invest. If the purchase saves you money in the long run, by all means, buy it. A fancy $25 lunch box to carry to work will save the purchase amount within a few days.

- Make saving a game. Think of ways you can cut spending or earn more. It's enjoyable watching your funds grow.

- Ask for discounts for cash. Some retailers even post signs that paying in cash will save you money. If not, ask especially for larger purchases. Also, some retailers and restaurants add 3% to your bill if you charge. Watch for signs before paying.

- Check your credit score. This number determines whether you'll be accepted for renting an apartment, purchasing a car, or qualifying for a credit card. The higher your credit score, the better your loan rate will likely be.

- Get rid of debt. The most crucial action is to get rid of debt, especially those pesky credit card balances with astronomical interest rates. Plenty of financial gurus can advise on how to achieve this. Everyone raves about Dave Ramsey and Charles Payne.

- Read more than one book on finances. There are many more ways to save and earn money than I can suggest here. Besides, I'm not a financial advisor. Educate yourself about how to protect your money.

- Build your savings in a high-interest savings account. Savings account returns vary drastically; online banks often pay higher rates than their counterpart brick-and-mortar institutions. Do your due diligence. Be sure to shop for the ones with good reputations and ratings.

- Open a high-interest savings account and spend only the interest. Never touch the principal nest egg.

- Don't succumb to those "no interest, pay it off in 6 months" deals. They get you at a 25% interest rate if you are one day late. It has happened to me, and I always pay on time. I've never charged a purchase that way since.

- Surely, you know about credit card points that can be turned into cash, gift cards for merchandise, pay on your account balance, or travel and hotels. These add up quickly. Don't get carried away and charge monthly amounts you can't pay off.

- Cut back on your spending. Ideas include having a drink or two at home instead of going out or visiting museums and tourist attractions on free days.

- Always get your employer's 401K match. This is free money that you should take advantage of and max out.

- Improve your skills to advance in your job or get a new one. You'll become better at what you do, and the position of your dreams might be in your future.

- Spend money on experiences rather than material things. Your memories of experiences tend to last longer than the lifespan of your new shoes.

- Think differently about the concept of retirement and think more in terms of financial independence. Retirement might be a long way off for some, and it might be hard to wrap your head around it so far in the distance. Financial Independence or Retire Early (FIRE) is an approach where people plan to retire much earlier than usual by committing to extreme saving and investing. However, I am not suggesting that you follow such extreme measures or retire early. Instead, a modified approach is to increase your saving and investment habits early on in life, which can help you build a substantial nest egg much faster without sacrificing everything you find enjoyable.

Think of it as saving for an exotic vacation in a few years. You'll have several years of savings banked when your vacation rolls around. By viewing it this way, you will likely feel more motivated to work towards your goal. You will be surprised how fast the interest adds up, and you'll have peace of mind with more bucks in the bank.

Additionally, you may not know what you want to do when you reach retirement age. You may start a new business or pursue a new hobby. Therefore, it is essential to have financial freedom so you can decide how to spend your money when the time comes. (Check with a financial adviser to determine the best approach for you.)

- Finally, it's okay if you get the itch to splurge occasionally. The main thing is to be aware of what you are doing. You could set aside money every week/month to contribute to a fund just for the time you need to treat yourself. You are less likely to have buyer's remorse if the money is earmarked. No matter how you allocate for the splurges, save your receipts if the purchase doesn't seem to hold the expectations you thought it would. You may rather have the money in the bank instead.

Chapter 9

Embracing Gratitude

Cultivating a Luxury Mindset

Every day, I pass by a framed picture in my office that reads,

"Gratitude turns what we have into enough."

Think about this for a moment. The daily habit of practicing gratitude is a powerful tool. By appreciating the good things in your life, such as your loved ones, your surroundings, and your world, you train yourself to be grateful for even the smallest of joys, such as a blue sky, sitting on the porch listening to the rain, or the sound of someone you love calling your name. Fostering a habit of gratitude can help you stay positive during challenging times, when you face obstacles, or when life takes an unexpected turn.

Gratitude changes your perspective. Expressing gratitude is a beautiful feeling that stems from being aware of the good things in life and feeling thankful for them. It's a positive emotion that can brighten our day and help us appreciate what we have.

What you have is enough when you are thankful—no more yearning for a new car or longing for a beautiful home in a plush neighborhood. You would be content with your weight, job, and partner at any given time and most everything in your life. How would you feel about that? It doesn't mean you can't strive for more; simply be mindful of the blessings you have now.

Have you ever noticed how being grateful for all your life's good things can fill you with positive energy? It's like a regenerative force that makes you feel fulfilled and content. The best part is that when you face obstacles and difficulties, this positive energy can help you transform those adversities into opportunities for growth and development. It's like a superpower that we all have access to!

Gratitude frees you from negative thoughts to fuel resiliency in life's journey. Not only does it make you happier, but it can also improve your health, relationships, and overall resilience. So why not take a moment today to thank someone for their kindness or appreciate something good in your life? It's a small gesture that can have a significant impact! It's amazing how much brighter everything becomes when we approach it with gratitude. Practicing gratitude can transform our outlook on life and help us appreciate all the good surrounding us.

When the day's activities don't go my way, it is easy to drop into a bad mood and forget about all the blessings within my reach, like air conditioning on a sweltering day or warmth in my beautiful home as I watch the snow swirling outside. Or how about clean running water with a tap of the fixture? How can I forget about all of the people who love me? I'll run out of space before I can list a fraction of my blessings.

For years, I have been writing down five things I am grateful for in my gratitude journal before I go to bed each night. I rarely miss a night. Framing your thoughts before bed is essential because it sets you up with positive thoughts for the night and gives you a better night's sleep. Make this your priority on the list that follows.

- Keep a gratitude journal. Write five things you are grateful for every evening before bed.

- Take a moment to appreciate the moment at any given time. With practice, you'll feel grateful in moments you would not normally consider your best. If you think there is nothing to be thankful for, consider that "things could always be worse." Besides, I often find that something good comes from less-than-desirable circumstances: a lesson learned, a new opportunity, or a disaster averted. The secret is standing in gratitude no matter what and being patient long enough to see the reward.

- Look for the glimmer of hope. You'll always find the bright side of any situation when you look hard enough. Although it may not be immediate, it will appear. You lost the promotion, but a better job came from a timely recruiter phone call. You missed a flight but were seated in first class on the next one. You struggled through a miserable breakup, but you found the love of your life.

- Appreciate the things you have rather than see what you don't have.

- Make the menial tasks enjoyable with gratitude. One day, it occurred to me how much better my life would be if I made an effort to love all the jobs I had to do throughout the day. I would stop grumbling and appreciate that I could and had the opportunity to do them. It crossed my mind that I am beyond fortunate to have beautiful blessings, particularly a lovely house and yard that require much of my time to keep them looking well-kept. We are expected to be good stewards of those things given to us, and at that moment, my attitude toward them changed 180 degrees.

Whatever we are
waiting for – peace
of mind, contentment,
grace, the inner
awareness of simple
abundance – it will
surely come to us,
but only when we
are ready to receive
it with an open and
grateful heart.

~ Sarah Ban Breathnach

- Be of service. Showing your gratitude daily is as simple as being of service to someone, saying a kind word, holding the door open, or handwriting a note of thanks. Serving someone is the best way to get out of a rotten mood. It takes you away from thinking about yourself and on to helping others in some way. This outreach also circles to attracting abundance.

- Be patient. Patience is a strength that improves your ability to successfully work through life's challenges as you are experiencing them. It allows you self-control in reacting to the situation. Sometimes, the blessings take time to manifest, and patience will enable us to stay focused on continuing to do the work. Don't waste any of your life wishing that time will pass quickly until you get what you want. Life is fleeting enough.

Connie Paradise

112

Chapter 10

Adopting an Abundance Mindset

Manifesting Luxury

There is a difference between living an abundant life and having a luxurious lifestyle. Abundance is attached to comfort, harmony, peace, and beauty, while luxury is attached to temporary material possessions. Abundantly means living in gratitude without fear or limitation. An abundance mindset is an optimistic frame of mind that focuses on what we have rather than what we don't have.

Gratitude is harmonious with abundance. By concentrating on motivation instead of fear, we can attract what we want and open ourselves up to endless opportunities. You start recognizing the blessings that come your way every day. A mindset of abundance brings positivity and happiness not only to yourself but also to those around you. Through hard work, determination, and belief that the sky is the limit, there is no end to your success and joy.

Expressing gratitude is essential to attract abundance. Gratitude strengthens your ability to manifest your desires. Let me explain how gratitude and abundance are intertwined.

While many of us have heard of the Universal Law of Attraction, other laws also play a role in our lives. We'll look at how the three laws are both dependent and interdependent on one another.

According to the Law of Attraction, positive thoughts and actions will result in favorable outcomes, whereas negativity can lead to negative consequences. The Law of Abundance states an endless supply of resources, wealth, and opportunities are available to everyone. Furthermore, the Law of Vibration suggests that everything in the universe consists of energy that vibrates at varying frequencies. This energy attracts similar frequencies, including our thoughts, emotions, and beliefs, which vibrate at their unique frequencies.

There is much to learn about the flow of energy, but I'll stick to the fundamentals for this book. Vibration is an essential element for achieving positivity in life. By understanding its significance, you can use it to create a fulfilling and meaningful existence. The Law of Vibration

114

states that all matter vibrates continuously, generating energy. To quote Albert Einstein, "Everything in life is vibration."

Understanding the power of vibration is the key to a gratifying life. You can create a life full of meaning and purpose by tapping into its energy. Once you realize that everything in the universe is made up of vibrations, it becomes clear that the self and the world are not separate entities but different expressions of a single, unchanging reality. This interconnectedness means that everything is ultimately connected and part of the same whole.

Once you understand this powerful Law and can incorporate it into your everyday life, your reality will change dramatically.

The speed or rate at which something vibrates is referred to as its frequency," with the only difference between one object and another being the rate of its vibration. Your body vibrates at a frequency at different levels, with fear, anger, and scarcity being very low on the scale and gratitude vibrating around the level of love. Vibration attracts like vibrations, so you'll get more of the same when your body vibrates at low levels. Conversely, when your body vibrates at a higher frequency, you will attract more of the same.

Maintaining a positive mindset requires being aware of your emotional state. Recognizing negative thoughts can help you shift your perspective, especially in difficult or disappointing situations. Sometimes, it's necessary to be patient and wait for the right time or a better opportunity. Regardless, it's essential to keep your vibrations high.

When you practice gratitude and focus on abundance, you attract more positivity. We can attract more of what we desire by acting from a place of motivation and abundance instead of fear and scarcity. The reality is that there are endless opportunities and resources in the world for everyone. When we wish abundance for others, too, it helps us to cultivate this way of thinking, and the Universe will respond accordingly. Embrace abundance for a luxuriant life, not lack.

Practice these daily prompts and notice how you and the things around you change.

- Begin with gratitude. Be thankful for what you have now.

- Dream it. Write your vision so precisely that you know all the details, whether they have happened or not. Go after it fearlessly.

- Mind your mind. Be aware of what you are thinking. Shift your mind to think positively about what you want. Remove all limiting thoughts.

- Speak positively. Rather than saying, "I'll never have the money," say, "I'll buy this at another time."

Vibrational Energy Chart

Creative Energy

Destructive Energy

- Expect blessings. God wants you to be blessed. When you expect and believe they will be coming, they surely will. They may arrive outside your time frame, but it will be when the time is right.

- See challenges as opportunities to grow. There will always be challenges. Focus on what is working well for you.

- Dump toxic relationships. You only get one life. Surround yourself with people who share your beliefs and support you. It's okay to let go.

- Offer a smile to someone. If you have never smiled at someone you don't know at the grocery

117

store, you might be surprised to learn that their face lights up. Sometimes, the simplest acts of kindness, like a smile, can make a big difference. I've done it thousands of times and found it does more good for me than it does for them. You never know what kind of day they've had or the life they are living.

- Think abundance, not lack. By shifting our minds to act through motivation rather than fear, we attract more of what we want. The world has unlimited opportunities and resources. Wanting more for others helps to put us in this mindset. Understand that there is plenty for all. The Universe will respond in kind when you want more for others.

- Attract more of what you want. If you want more love, give more of it. More money? Be more generous. More appreciation? Praise someone. Improve a skill? Practice it. You will attract what you think. Focus on the good.

- Reach for the stars. Be honest with yourself and go for your dream. There's a good chance you won't be your happiest unless you do.

- Stop making excuses. There's always a way. You just haven't thought of it yet. You will find a way if your desire is strong enough. There are trillions of stories about people who have overcome unbelievable situations against overwhelming odds. What will you do to make your dream a reality? Commit to it.

- Wish for peace, joy, and prosperity for all. Wishing authentic peace, happiness, and prosperity for others elevates your vibration beyond financial gain to emotional, mental, physical, and spiritual well-being.

Above all, it is important to forgive those who have caused you pain. You can't reap abundance without forgiving. Anger and shame lower your body's vibration to attract more of the same. When someone hurts you, typically, it's all you can think about for days. It rears its ugly head over and over when you least expect it. They've gone on with their life, not giving you a single thought while leaving you to dwell on it for heaven knows how long.

Forgiving can release you from the grip of the person who has harmed you. In some cases, forgiveness may even result in a sense of empathy, compassion, and understanding for the individual who hurt you. However, it's important to note that forgiving someone doesn't mean forgetting or excusing the harm they caused. You don't have to remain friends, partners, or acquaintances. Simply forgive them and carry on. You will be happy you did.

Appreciate where you are
at every stage of your life.
Don't waste a second
wishing you were somebody
or somewhere else.

Epilogue

I couldn't leave you without sharing these final thoughts. I've learned these valuable lessons after much trial and error. They have served me well and reaped much happiness and joy.

- Helping someone is the best mood lifter.

- Stop expecting your happiness to come from other people. Happiness is a luxury you create yourself.

- Stay off social media. Ignore curated posts that exaggerate lifestyles. If you must scroll, recognize that they aren't always what they seem.

- Stop worrying. Most of the things you worry about never happen.

- Stop regretting the past. You can't change it. Learn from it and move on.

- Live in the moment. Slow down occasionally and notice the butterflies.

- Pick your relationships. Get rid of those that aren't working for you. It's okay.

- Celebrate your wins. Always have a split of champagne on hand.

- Try new things. It keeps life exciting and worth living.

- Take risks. You have a 100% chance of not succeeding if you don't step out.

- Get 10 minutes of sunshine every morning. It gives you the recommended amount of Vitamin D, reactivates your day, and helps you sleep better at night.

- Slow down and savor the moment. This is hard because I want to accomplish so much and have many experiences.

- Always, always insist on quality over quantity. This goes for food, clothes, experiences, friends, and anything else you can think of.

- Don't miss an opportunity to tell someone you love them.

I hope you enjoyed reading this book as much as I did writing it. Most of all, I hope you put lots of these ideas into practice. There are times now that I wish I had slowed life down and appreciated the moment rather than rushing on to the next thing, but I didn't until a few years ago. Looking back, I see that my journey was remarkable and much more than I ever dreamed.

One of my favorite quotes comes from a French author and journalist who wrote the novella Gigi. She sums it up beautifully.

> *"What a wonderful life I've had! I only*
> *wish that I had realized it sooner!"*
> *~Sidonie Gabriel Collette*

Life is too short to waste it on the same old routines. If you truly desire change, it's time to step out of your comfort zone and face the fear. Take a risk, try something new, and even if you fail, know you are one step closer to success. Don't just wish for a better life; actively pursue it. Stop complaining and start taking action. You have the power to create the life you want, so go out there and make it happen!

I wish you blessings, good fortune, and an abundantly prosperous, luxurious life lived with intention.

Guide for Simple Luxury

Thanks!

To Ollin Toler, the love of my life, who believes in and encourages me daily to let my light shine.

To Crystel Lynn Smith, who set me on the road to writing this book.

To Tamara Wolfe, who changed my heart and jump-started my thoughts to paper.

To my Mastermind Group, Karen Estrin, Kathie York, and Bill Searles, for their brilliant suggestions, endless help, and support. To Kathie for coming up with the title. To Karen, who coached me through the rough spots.

To Robin Bowers, my sister, who loyally listens to me grumble when necessary.

To Katie Rossman, my dear friend, who says, "It's a Connie thing to do" whenever I launch myself into the latest project.

To Bidy Carroll, my dear friend who thinks I can do anything and makes me roar with laughter even in the most dreadful situations.

To Melinda Gipson, who graciously gave her editing expertise.

To Lisa Talbott, who helped me with the finer points of my message.

To Danita Roble, who helps me keep my head on straight.

To Meredith Hancock, who is forever patient no matter how often I call for help.

Notes

1. Forbes.com, "Why We Buy More Than We Need, "https://www.forbes.com/sites/joshuabecker/2018/11/27/why-we-buy-more-than-we-need/?sh=359816526417 (accessed September 22, 2023).

2. CNBC.com, "Buying Luxury Items Makes You Feel Less Confident and Authentic, study says," Cory Stieg, Dec 30 20199:01 AM EST https://www.cnbc.com/2019/12/27/study-buying-luxury-items-makes-you-feel-less-confident-and-authentic.html. (accessed September 22, 2023)

3. WebMD.com, "How Clutter Can Affect Your Health," Medically Reviewed by, on August 28, 2023, Written by Barbara Brody https://www.webmd.com/balance/ss/slideshow-clutter-affects-health (accessed September 27, 2023

RESOURCES

Stores to Shop
Wayfair
Overstock
Ruggables
Home Goods
Target
Etsy
The Container Store
Chartreuse
Linen Locker
Lowes
Hobby Lobby
Michaels

References
Houzz
Veranda
Food and Wine

Courses
Domestika
Masterclass

The Author

Connie Paradise is a photographer, mother, grandmother, and wife to Ollin Toler. She retired from a thirty-year career in association management in Washington, DC, and pursued her love for creativity through photography. Her photographic journey began in 2015 when she focused on professional women showing their grace, beauty, and strength through her lens so they could see the beauty in their curves, flaws, and uniqueness.

Connie has a natural talent for design and organization and sometimes can be found rearranging her living room in the wee hours of the morning. She shares economical tips and ideas for making your home and lifestyle more organized, elevated, and enjoyable on her blog, APeekAtParadise.com.

Connie and Ollin moved to Winchester, VA, from Northern Virginia the day before they were married in 2017 and have been renovating their home project-by-project ever since.

Sons Stefan and Jared have families of their own. Their two cats, Leonard and Loretta, keep them entertained.

Made in the USA
Middletown, DE
21 February 2024